COUNTRY EXPLORERS

MEXICO

Lerner Publications Company • Minneapolis

The editor wishes to thank Juana Inés Dehesa Christlieb for her careful review of this book.

Lerner Publications Company
A division of Lerner Publishing Group, Inc.
241 First Avenue North
Minneapolis, MN 55401 U.S.A.

Website address: www.lernerbooks.com

Library of Congress Cataloging-in-Publication Data

Streissguth, Thomas, 1958–
    Mexico / by Tom Streissguth.
      p. cm. — (Country explorers)
    Includes index.
    ISBN: 978–0–8225–7130–8 (lib. bdg. : alk. paper)
    1. Mexico—Geography—Juvenile literature. I. Title.
  F1408.9.S77 2008
  917.2—dc22   2006036726

Manufactured in the United States of America
1 2 3 4 5 6 – JR – 13 12 11 10 09 08

Table of Contents

Welcome!	4	Work	30
Coast to Coast	6	Faith	33
Traveling	8	Sports	34
In the Valley	10	Story Time	36
In the South	13	Pictures	39
Mexicans	14	Music	40
First Peoples	16	Crafts	42
Family	18	*The Flag of Mexico*	*44*
Neighborhoods	20	*Fast Facts*	*45*
Food	22	*Glossary*	*46*
Market	24	*To Learn More*	*47*
Fiesta!	26	*Index*	*48*
School	28		

Welcome!

All aboard! We're crossing a river called the Rio Grande to the country of Mexico. At the border, the river is called the Río Bravo.

Mexico sits on the continent of North America. The United States lies north of Mexico. Belize and Guatemala are south of Mexico. On a map, Mexico looks a bit like a giant ice-cream cone.

The Rio Grande winds along the border between Mexico and the United States.

MILES
0   200
0   200
KILOMETERS

mountains
deserts
plains
rain forests
valleys
volcanoes
country's capital

Mexico

RÍO GRANDE
RÍO BRAVO

SIERRA MADRE ORIENTAL

MEXICO

PÁNUCO RIVER

VALLEY
OF
MEXICO

Mexico City

Iztaccíhuatl

LERMA RIVER

Popocatépetl

Orizaba

GULF
OF
MEXICO

YUCATÁN
PENINSULA

SIERRA MADRE DEL SUR

BALSAS RIVER

N

PACIFIC
OCEAN

BELIZE

GAUTEMALA

HONDURAS

Coast to Coast

Water is on almost every side of Mexico. The Pacific Ocean meets the country's western coast. On the eastern side of Mexico lies a big circle of water. It is called the Gulf of Mexico.

The Pacific Ocean laps Mexico's western coastline. The Pacific is the largest ocean in the world.

Mexico has just about every kind of land. It has tropical rain forests and flat land called plains. It has mountains and dry deserts. It even has snowy mountaintops! Orizaba is Mexico's highest mountain. Orizaba has snow on it all year.

Map Whiz Quiz

Take a look at the map on pages 4 and 5. A map is a drawing or chart of a place. Trace the outline of Mexico onto a sheet of paper. See if you can find the Pacific Ocean. Mark this side of your map with a *W* for west. How about the Gulf of Mexico? Mark this side with an *E* for east. Color in the regions labeled Baja California and Yucatán. These areas are called peninsulas. Peninsulas are pieces of land with water on three sides.

Mountains and deserts are part of Mexico's landscape. This desert is in Baja California.

Traveling

Mexicans travel from place to place in many different ways. Some ways are fast. Others are slow. Cars speed along busy roads. Trucks and buses zoom by too.

The streets in Mexico City have a lot of traffic.

Mexico's trains bring busy travelers from place to place.

Trains chug across plains and through valleys. Airplanes crisscross the skies above. Some people in Mexico travel by donkey. If you were in Mexico, what kind of ride would you choose?

In the Valley

In the middle of Mexico are two sets of mountains. One set is called the Sierra Madre Occidental. The other is known as the Sierra Madre Oriental. Between them is a flat piece of land. This land is called the Valley of Mexico. The valley is home to Mexico City.

The Copper Canyon is in the Sierra Madre Occidental.

Mexico City is very large. Long ago, Native Mexicans called Aztecs also built cities in this valley. Then people from Spain crossed the Atlantic Ocean. They took over the Aztecs and their land. The Spaniards built their own cities.

¡Hola!

Today we took a train ride through the Copper Canyon. We started at Chihuahua (the city, not the dog!) and ended at Los Mochis, a town on the western coast. Mountains and cliffs rose on both sides of the train tracks. At times, steep, scary drop-offs appeared right next to the train. I closed my eyes when that happened. Tomorrow we're taking a boat ride to Baja. Wish you were here!

¡Adios, Amigos!

Your

Your

Anywh

Mexico City

Popocatépetl reaches high into the sky.

In the South

Giant twin volcanoes rise south of Mexico City. One is named Popocatépetl. That means "smoking mountain" in the Aztec language. The other volcano is Iztaccíhuatl. That means "white woman."

The Sierra Madre del Sur stand south of the volcanoes. Nearby is a rain forest. The rain forest is home to many spider monkeys. Mangoes and other fruits also thrive there.

Many plants and animals live in Mexico's lush rain forests.

13

Mexicans

At one time, Native Mexicans were the only people in Mexico. Then Spain took over. Spanish people moved to Mexico. Many of these people married Native Mexicans. The children of these marriages are called mestizos.

Mexico is home to many different kinds of people. Its cities and towns are bustling places where people often gather.

Children in Mexico speak Spanish. They may also learn other languages in school.

The word *mestizo* means "mixed." Most Mexicans are mestizos. Most people who make their homes in Mexico speak Spanish.

15

First Peoples

Some parts of Mexico still have large numbers of Native Mexicans. The Maya live in southern Mexico. So do the Mixtec and the Zapotec.

Young Mayans in Cozumel. Cozumel is an island off the coast of the Yucatán Peninsula.

16

The Seri live in the dry
northern states. The Seri
move from place to place.
They travel to find food and
water. Some Native Mexicans
speak little Spanish. They use
their own languages.

A Native Mexican
man wears
traditional clothing.

Family

Family life is very important in Mexico. Some Mexican households are small. Others are large. They might have three, four, or more children.

A Mexican family rests on a bench in a Cancún shopping mall.

18

Some families share their homes with relatives. Children might live with their aunts, uncles, cousins, and grandparents. Grandparents help with chores. They also watch the children. Grown-up sons and daughters take care of family members as they get older.

Family Words

Here are the Spanish words for family members.

father	padre	(PAH-dray)
mother	madre	(MAH-dray)
uncle	tío	(TEE-oh)
aunt	tía	(TEE-ah)
grandfather	abuelo	(ah-BWAY-loh)
grandmother	abuela	(ah-BWAY-lah)
son	hijo	(EE-hoh)
daughter	hija	(EE-hah)
brother	hermano	(her-MAH-noh)
sister	hermana	(her-MAH-nah)

Grandparents, aunts, uncles, and cousins might all help to care for their family's youngest members.

19

Neighborhoods

The streets in Mexican cities are lively. *¡Hola!* People shout as they say hello to their friends on the sidewalks. Honk! Cars, buses, and motor scooters rush by on the roads. Home is a good place to get away from the noise.

The city of San Cristóbal de las Casas is in the Mexican state of Chiapas. It is a very busy place.

Brightly colored homes line many Mexican streets.

Some Mexican homes are made of stone. They might have quiet courtyards in the center. Many city families live in tall apartment buildings. In Mexican towns and villages, homes are often made of clay bricks. These bricks are called adobe. In Yucatán, the Mayans build houses out of tree branches and grass.

Food

¡Picante! Mexican food is spicy. That's what picante means. Many Mexicans use hot chili peppers to season their foods. Mexicans have been growing chili peppers for thousands of years. They grow many other crops too.

Hot chili peppers add spice and flavor to many foods.

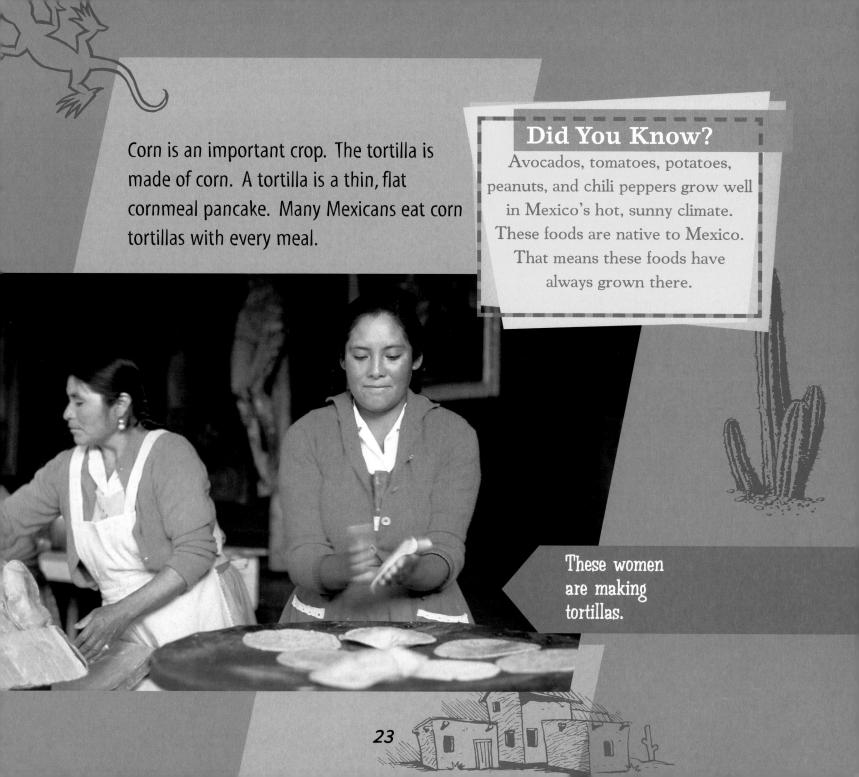

Corn is an important crop. The tortilla is made of corn. A tortilla is a thin, flat cornmeal pancake. Many Mexicans eat corn tortillas with every meal.

These women are making tortillas.

23

Mexican markets bustle with activity.

Market

Many Mexicans shop at outdoor markets. The markets open early. They stay open all day. Shoppers can buy food, clothing, jewelry—almost everything they need.

In small towns, farmers bring their extra crops to sell at the local market. They weigh the fruits and vegetables on scales for customers. The farmers may also have chickens, ducks, or turkeys for sale.

Shoppers at this market in Oaxaca have many colorful fruits and vegetables to choose from.

25

Fiesta!

In Mexico, a special party is called a fiesta. During a fiesta, schools close. Work stops. Everyone in town meets at the plaza. They have a fun time. Bands play. People laugh and sing. They wave to their friends.

Fiestas are times for people to enjoy being with their friends and family.

Piñatas hang from trees or ceilings. Piñatas are pretty containers full of treats. Blindfolded children take turns trying to break open the piñata with a wooden stick. Then the goodies fall out. People shout. Fireworks go off. The celebration may last for a full day or even two! Nobody gets much sleep during a fiesta.

Day of the Dead

Every year, on November 2, Mexicans celebrate the Day of the Dead. This holiday is a time to remember family members who have died. Families bring food and flowers to honor these relatives. At night, the family brings candles. They set up a picnic near their relatives' graves. But the Day of the Dead isn't sad. It's a celebration!

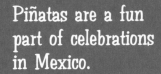

Piñatas are a fun part of celebrations in Mexico.

School

Mexican children attend preschool. They also go to kindergarten. After kindergarten, the children go to elementary school.

School-age children pose for a picture in the Mexican state of Yucatán.

Many Mexican schools have new equipment, such as computers. But some schools in poor areas have only a room and desks. In these parts of Mexico, some children go to school for just a few years. Others don't go at all. These kids need to work at home or on their family's farm.

Some Mexican schools have outdoor classrooms.

29

Work

Mexicans have many different kinds of jobs. Some people have service jobs. They work in restaurants or hotels. Mexico has warm weather and pretty beaches. People like to travel there. As a result, Mexico has lots of service jobs.

These women work as cooks in a restaurant.

Other Mexicans work in industry. They might make cars, clothing, or other things. Mexico sets aside some land especially for factories. This land is near the United States. U.S. companies set up lots of factories on this land. So many Mexicans work in factories. Still other Mexicans work on farms. They make money by growing crops. But Mexico does not have enough jobs for everyone. Some Mexicans leave the country to find work.

This Mayan father and son work on a farm in Quintana Roo, a state on the Yucatán Peninsula.

The Cathedral Metropolitana is a famous Catholic church in Mexico City.

32

Faith

Most people in Mexico belong to the Roman Catholic Church. This was the church of the Spanish settlers. But some Native Mexicans have other religious beliefs.

The Tarahumara people worship the spirits of the sun, the moon, and the rain. The Maya and the Zapotec also practice old customs and beliefs.

December 12

December 12 is an important date in Mexico. On that day, Catholics honor the Virgin of Guadalupe. On December 12 in the year 1531, a Native Mexican named Juan Diego had a vision of Mary. Mary is the mother of Jesus. People built a church on the spot in Mexico City where Juan Diego had the vision. People who cannot travel to the church celebrate the day with fiestas in their own hometowns.

Soccer fans cheer on their favorite players in Mexico City's Olympic Stadium.

Sports

Mexicans love soccer! In Mexico, soccer is called *futbol*. Adults and children play futbol. They choose sides and set up goals in the streets, on playgrounds, and in soccer fields.

Wrestling is another popular sport. Many Mexicans watch *lucha libre*. Lucha libre is a special type of wrestling. In this sport, wrestlers called *luchadores* fight while wearing masks and colorful clothing. Luchadores wrestle on mats. They try to pin their opponents to the mat. Luchadores are heroes in Mexico.

El Santo

El Santo was one of Mexico's most popular luchadores. He was born in 1917. His real name was Rodolfo Guzmán Huerta. He used the name El Santo (the Saint) when he wrestled. El Santo was known for wearing a silver mask. It was part of his wrestling costume. He was also known for his film career. He starred in many movies. El Santo died in 1984. The people of Mexico were very sad.

Three luchadores pose in the wrestling ring.

Story Time

Mexico is a land of storytellers. Long ago, the Maya and Aztec people used pictures to tell stories about their peoples' histories.

Pictures that tell stories are called pictographs. Ancient pictographs cover the walls of some caves in Mexico.

In 1539, the first printing press in Mexico began making books in Mexico City. Since then, Mexico has made many different kinds of books.

An Aztec Tale

Would you like to hear an old Aztec story? This tale explains how the Aztecs came to be. A long time ago, all the world's human beings died in a flood. Later, the Aztec god Quetzalcoatl tricked the god who took care of the dead into giving him the dead people's bones. Quetzalcoatl ground the bones into a powder and mixed it with his own blood. He used this mixture to create the Aztecs.

This store in Guadalajara sells a wide variety of books.

A mural decorates the ceiling of the Government Palace in the city of Morelia.

Pictures

Another way of telling a story is through paintings. Murals are huge paintings on walls or ceilings.

Three well-known painters created many murals on the walls of important buildings in Mexico. These painters are José Clemente Orozco, David Alfaro Siqueiros, and Diego Rivera. By studying these painters' murals, you can learn more about Mexico's past.

Frida Kahlo

Frida Kahlo was another popular Mexican painter. She was born in Mexico City in 1907. Frida often painted portraits of herself. When she was a teenager, she was badly hurt in a bus accident. Many of her paintings show the pain she felt after her accident. Frida became famous for her paintings. She was also known for wearing colorful clothing. Frida was married to Diego Rivera, but they did not always get along. Frida died in 1954.

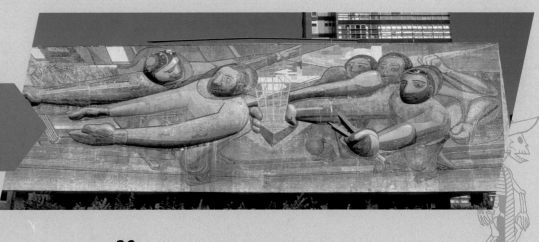

David Alfaro Siqueiros created this mural on a building in Mexico City.

Music

The weather is often warm in Mexico. So many Mexicans spend lots of time outside. They might listen to music while enjoying the warm weather. In some towns, concerts take place on Sunday nights in the plaza. Street bands play Mexican folk music.

Music is an important part of Mexican culture.

Mariachi is one type of folk music. Mariachi bands dress in *charro* clothing. This clothing is a traditional outfit of cowboys.

Flying Dancers

Native Mexicans called Totonacs take part in a ceremony known as the Voladores. In the ceremony, four men climb up a high pole. They tie themselves to ropes that are wrapped around the pole. Then the men jump head first into the air. No kidding! The ropes unwind. The men slowly twist their way to the ground. At the last minute, the men turn right side up. They land on their feet.

A mariachi band plays in the state of Jalisco.

Crafts

Artists in Mexico make crafts by hand. Then they sell the crafts. You can buy them in the plazas, at the marketplace, and on the streets. Potters, weavers, jewelers, basket makers, and wood-carvers make pots, rugs, and necklaces. They make kitchen tools and wall hangings too.

Beautiful carpets are just one of many craft items that you can find in Mexico.

Some cities are known for certain crafts. People in the southern city of Puebla make brightly painted tiles. These are called talavera tiles. People use talavera tiles to decorate buildings.

Blue, green, and yellow talavera tiles bring color to the Templo de San Francisco. This church is in the state of Puebla.

43

THE FLAG OF MEXICO

Mexico's flag is green, white, and red. The green stripe stands for hope. The white stripe stands for purity. The red stripe stands for the blood of Mexico's heroes. An eagle sits in the middle of the flag. The eagle is an Aztec symbol. An old story says that the Aztecs saw an eagle at the place where they built the city of Tenochtitlán. The eagle is perched on a cactus with red fruit. The fruit stands for the human heart. Beneath the eagle are some branches. The branches on the right represent victory. The branches on the left represent strength.

FAST FACTS

FULL COUNTRY NAME: United Mexican States

AREA: 759,529 square miles (1,953,162 square kilometers), or slightly less than three times the size of Texas

MAIN LANDFORMS: the mountain Orizaba; the mountain ranges Sierra Madre Occidental, Sierra Madre Oriental, and Sierra Madre del Sur; the valley Valley of Mexico; the volcanoes Popocatépetl and Iztaccíhuatl

MAJOR RIVERS: Río Bravo, Pánuco, Lerma, Balsas

ANIMALS AND THEIR HABITATS: spider monkeys (rain forest), quetzals (rain forest), gray whales (ocean), Gila monsters (desert)

CAPITAL CITY: Mexico City

OFFICIAL LANGUAGE: Spanish

POPULATION: about 107,449,525

GLOSSARY

continent: any one of seven large areas of land. The continents are Africa, Antarctica, Asia, Australia, Europe, North America, and South America.

desert: a dry, sandy region

fiesta: a special party

map: a drawing or chart of all or part of Earth or the sky

mestizo: a person with both Spanish and Native Mexican ancestry. Most people in Mexico are mestizos.

mountain: a part of Earth's surface that rises high into the sky

mural: a huge painting on a wall or ceiling

peninsula: a piece of land with water on three sides

piñata: a pretty container full of treats. Blindfolded children take turns trying to break open a piñata with a wooden stick.

plain: a large area of flat land

rain forest: a thick, green forest that gets lots of rain every year

valley: a low-lying piece of land between hills or mountains. *Valley* can also mean "an area of land that gets its water from a large river."

volcano: an opening in Earth's surface through which hot, melted rock shoots up. *Volcano* can also refer to the hill or mountain of ash and rock that builds up around the opening.

TO LEARN MORE

BOOKS

Krebs, Laurie, and Christopher Corr. *Off We Go to Mexico! An Adventure in the Sun*. Cambridge, MA: Barefoot Books, 2006. This fun book tells the story of a family's trip to Mexico.

Lowery, Linda. *Day of the Dead*. Minneapolis: Carolrhoda Books, 2004. Read all about the Day of the Dead, a special time in Mexico for celebrating life and honoring people who have died.

Marx, David F. *Mexico*. New York: Children's Press, 2000. Learn more about the geography and culture of Mexico.

Winter, Jonah. *Diego*. New York: Knopf Books for Young Readers, 2007. This picture book is written in both English and Spanish. It tells the story of Diego Rivera, the talented Mexican muralist.

WEBSITES

Mexico
http://www.timeforkids.com/TFK/specials/goplaces/0,12405,176084,00.html
This website from the magazine *Time for Kids* features virtual tours to Mexico, a guide to Spanish phrases, a quiz about Mexico, and more.

México for Kids
http://www.elbalero.gob.mx/index_kids.html
Visit this site to read more about Mexico's land and people. You can also try some fun activities and games.

INDEX

arts and crafts, 38–39, 42–43
Aztecs, 11, 36–37

families, 18–19
fiestas, 26–27
food, 22–25

homes, 20–21

jobs, 30–31

map of Mexico, 4–5
Maya, 16, 21, 33, 36

mestizos, 14–15
Mexico City, 10–11, 13, 37
music, 40–41

rain forests, 7, 13
religion, 33

schools, 28–29
Seri, 17
sports, 34–35
storytelling, 36–37, 39

volcanoes, 12–13

The photographs in this book are used with the permission of: © John Elk III, pp. 4, 6, 7, 9, 21, 36, 42; © Robert Fried Photography/www.robertfriedphotography.com, pp. 8, 11, 14 (both), 15 (both), 18, 19, 22, 25, 26, 28, 30, 31, 37, 38, 39, 41; © Luther Linkhart/SuperStock, p. 10; © age fotostock/SuperStock, pp. 12, 13, 20; © Jeff Greenberg/Art Directors, p. 16; © Bildagentur-online.com/Art Directors, p. 17; © SuperStock, Inc./SuperStock, p. 23; © Prisma/SuperStock, pp. 24, 40; © Richard Cummins/SuperStock, p. 27; © Spencer Grant/Art Directors, p. 29; © Tibor Bognar/Art Directors, p. 32; © Paula Jansen, p. 33; © Geoff Dowen/Art Directors, p. 34; © Keith Dannemiller/KPA/ZUMA Press; p. 35; © Jan Butchofsky-Houser/CORBIS, p. 43.
Illustrations by © Bill Hauser/Independent Picture Service.

Cover: © Reuters/CORBIS.